HAU
LANCASTER COUNTY
PENNSYLVANIA

Ghosts and Other Strange Occurrences

By

Dorothy Burtz Fiedel

To Barbara, Best Wishes! [signature] 10/24/98

To My Mother

Dorothy Ella Smith Burtz
1918–1968

"In the night of death,
hope sees a star,
and listening love
can hear the rustle of a wing."[1]

Ingersoll

Table of Contents

Introduction

I am not one of those authors who will tell you I am a dyed-in-the-wool skeptic when it comes to ghosts or unexplained occurrences. Any writer or journalist who is even remotely human, cannot claim to be totally objective in his writing and be telling the truth. As soon as one consciously decides to use one word instead of another—"the snake crawled through the grass" rather than—"the snake slithered through the grass"—objectivity flies out the window. However, in the case of ghosts, seeing, hearing, smelling and being patted (rather abruptly) on the shoulder, is believing. And I am a believer.

The conversation around our dinner table in the evening may include a comment from my eldest son (age 21): "Oh, by the way, one of the 'girls' came to visit last night . . . I think it was Aunt Martha." We might discuss what color dress she had on, or how long she stood at the foot of his bed, but her appearance is nothing unusual . . . even though she passed away many years ago.

The conversation quickly turns to items of other interest. We live quite comfortably and happily with the ghosts in our home.

Millions of people down through the ages, all over the world have experienced what they interpreted to be "supernatural." Spirits, ghosts, specters—such a variety. They are kept alive by the telling and re-telling from person to person, one generation to the next.[1] Or in the case of a haunted house, one tenant to the next.

The sleepy towns along the Susquehanna River and surrounding areas in Lancaster County are rich in folklore, legend and active hauntings. Columbia, the home of my forebears, is particularly rich in supernatural and unexplained occurrences.

Even the Columbia Historic Preservation Society, located at 19 to 21 North Second Street, has its resident ghosts!

A stroll up Locust Street above Sixth Street in Columbia takes one past Mt. Bethel Cemetery. It is a truly ethereal sight when the early morning mist hangs heavy in the graveyard. One wonders how many residents who "don't believe in ghosts" have, over the years, on an evening stroll, quickened their gait or scooted across the street so they could pass at a "safer" distance.

Norwood has its "Headless Horseman."

Chickies has its "curse."

Miss Mary Mifflin still walks the grounds at her home in Norwood over a century after her death.

Initially, I had intended to write about "unusual sightings" in the tri-town area, Columbia, Marietta, and Mount Joy. But an ad run in one of the local papers generated a large response from all over Lancaster County, and I feel compelled to include some of these also.

Most of the following stories are first-hand accounts; that is the person who contacted me had the events happen to themselves. A few stories have been gleaned from newspaper accounts. Others are second-hand accounts, the events happening to family or friends of the people who were kind enough to share their story with me.

Some of the people I interviewed gave permission to use their name in connection with their story, others preferred to remain anonymous. Because of this some of the following stories list sources. In the stories from anonymous contributors, I have used fictitious names in telling their tale.

There was a common thread that seemed to connect all the people who contacted me. Each individual knew, beyond a shadow-of-a-doubt, that what happened to them was true. Many said they seldom talked about their experiences for fear of being ridiculed. Many said they were always skeptical of the supernatural until it happened to them.

If you are one of those who told me your story, I thank you very much. If your story isn't included in this book, it is only because I had such a large number of responses that I couldn't use them all. Possibly a second book may find yours among its pages.

Also included are a couple legends. Many versions have floated around over the years. Choosing the "correct" version was a difficult task . . . I hope I have succeeded.

For those of you who are skeptics and consider the appearance of a ghost or spirit of a departed (in other words . . . dead) individual an illusion, or hallucination of the mind, stop and look at the role the after-life has played throughout history.

One-fifth of the world's population have built their religion specifically around life after death. They are called Christians.[2]

Let any man, Protestant, Catholic, Jew or Mohammedan, or whatever, conscientiously say that there are no so-called "hidden meanings," no "miracles," no "mystical rites," no superstitions in their church-life somewhere, if not plentiful. What church or sect does not push some form or other of it upon its believers?[3]

Another argument supporting the existence of things we don't see but possibly only sense or feel can be made by reminding the skeptic of medical advances made in the relatively "recent" past. Louis Pasteur nearly got laughed out of Oxford University when he suggested to the greatest medical minds of his time that sickness and infection was caused by little, tiny animals, not visible to the human eye. The specter culprit is now commonly known as bacteria.

Lord Listern published his first paper on antisepsis (against infection) in surgery in 1867, two years after the end of America's Civil War.[4] The time lag between Europe and America in medical ideas meant that many of Union and Confederate soldiers died of disease and infection through injury that could have survived had the doctors of our armies been trained in the latest pathological discoveries. Even Harvard, America's finest medical school, had no stethoscope until 1868, thirty years after its invention, and no microscope until 1869, four years after the close of the Civil War.[5]

Disease? Putrification? Caused by something that's invisible but leaves its visible mark of infection . . . indeed! But view these organisms through the proper equipment and you've just dropped in on an active microscopic world.

Ghosts? Specters? The "life-force" of someone who has left their physical body and makes their presence known by turning on and off the lights, slamming doors, noisily tramping through the house and sometimes taking on a physical appearance . . . indeed! Possibly science has not developed the technology to view the world of the "spirit"; just as Harvard didn't have a microscope to view the fantastic world of microorganisms.

A Few Words About Ghosts and Haunted Houses

"It was a dark and stormy night (bear with me). The crashing thunder echoed through the valleys; the percussion rattled the rippled window panes of the clapboard house. Bright flashes of lightning illuminated the dark recesses of the wooden porch making the dancing shadows of the swaying branches disappear for a breathless moment. As the automobile crept to a halt another piercing flash lit the fuzzy shadow standing motionless in the front yard of the eerie wooden house. 'FOR SALE', it said."

This is the stuff of which "B" movies are made.

Haunted houses. How many of us remember having one in their town when they were children? The house that seemed dark, lifeless. The owners who were never home or if they were, were never seen. Curtains that hung limp, only to move to reveal an unfamiliar visage . . . not the owner, but the un-dead who had the run of the place.

People who own haunted houses are sometimes reluctant to speak on the record about their own haunted adobe. They fear ridicule, unwanted visits by curious ghost-seekers, or worse yet, decreased market value of their property.[1]

"Ghosts are like termites. If they're there, you have to disclose them," said one Lancaster County real estate agent in an October, 1992, *Lancaster Sunday News* article.[2]

"But you don't put up a sign that says, 'haunted house'. Although, if you did, you'd probably have to have more showings."[3]

One real estate agent that I spoke to said, "We have to reveal if

5

a house is 'stigmatized'. For instance, if there was a murder or suicide take place in the home we must tell the prospective buyer."

This author, and probably also you, the reader, would be very hesitant about buying a home where someone in the recent past swung half-mast from the balcony or did some organic redecorating with a strategically placed gunshot blast.

But what would these ghosts look like? According to Harry Shepherd, a physic researcher from Mission Viejo, California, "They are transparent entities, and if they don't want to be seen, they don't have to be seen."[4]

Harry Shepherd has seen ghosts—even nodded to them—at funerals as they sat beside their weeping widows in mortuaries and graveyards, a transparent arm slung over a loved one's hunched, heaving shoulders. He has watched as they make their way among the mourners, milky images of the departed honed in on hushed confidences. Eight out of ten of those who pass from this world, Shepherd believes, hang around for a few days to ease-drop on their own funerals.[5]

This ghost "expert," who has a doctorate in metaphysical science from the Universal Life Church in Phoenix, Arizona says, "Every house has spirits in it; ghosts are cool spots in the hall, fuzzy figures amid the antiques or unexplained sounds in the next room. Spotting ghosts, according to Shepherd, is seeing something out of the corner of your eye. Most people will think they've seen something, then dismiss it.[6]

Some of the most frequent phrases that I have heard while interviewing people for this book were, "I saw something out of the corner of my eye," or ". . . it was a shadow that darted across the room," or ". . . I had a strange feeling that someone or something was there." This visual vagueness sometimes gave way to more concrete occurrences.

Distinct odors, loud footsteps, slamming doors, electrical appliances turning on and off, objects disappearing and reappearing, voices, cold spots, or windless breezes may all be indicators of an unexplained presence occupying the space between four walls.

But if the fear of "new ghosts" can lower the value of a property; the "genteel old-ghost" may increase its value.[7]

6

There is an undeniable element of romance in a haunting. A ghost who lives in the reality of a century long past still searching for a lost love, a buried treasure, refusing to leave a slot in time where happiness or heart break still grips its spirit, or just hangs around because it likes it there, adds an appealing, mysterious charm to an old building.

The White House, in Washington, D.C., is reported to be haunted.[8] Queen Wilhelmina of the Netherlands is said to have opened her door one night to a strange knock while an overnight guest of Franklin D. Roosevelt. Much to her surprise she saw the ghost of Abraham Lincoln standing there. The next morning she told her host, F.D.R. of her experience. He said he wasn't surprised because his wife had also experienced something strange. Mrs. Roosevelt saw Lincoln several times, sometimes in the Oval Office Room. Mrs. Calvin Coolidge is said to have seen him there also.[9]

Dolly Madison still walks the grounds of the White House. Her most emphatic appearance is recorded as having occurred when the second Mrs. Woodrow Wilson ordered the White House gardeners to move Dolly's rose garden. In all her early nineteenth century fashions and furbelows, President Madison's wife flounced up to the gardeners and gave them a thorough tongue lashing. They then and there desisted, and the rose garden remains exactly where it always was.[10]

Of course, few of the buildings in Lancaster County are as well known or have been occupied by such high profile, public figures in history. But each home, no matter how humble or how grand, at one time sheltered the human spirit; and each is a king in his own castle.

As humans, death is as inevitable and as natural an act as being born, for the human body is not immortal. The spirit however, just may linger. And who knows, maybe that *was* Elvis I spotted in K-Mart. . . .

Albert Einstein on the Mysterious

Mystery exists within our natural, everyday world. Our minds, faced with these mysteries, can experience confusion, a most disturbing and difficult state of mind. Possibly, the mysteries should be viewed in the same light as Albert Einstein viewed them:

> "The most beautiful and most profound emotion we can experience is the sensation of the mystical. It is the sower of all true science. He to whom this emotion is a stranger, who can no longer wonder and stand rapt in awe, is as good as dead. To know that what is impenetrable to us really exists, manifesting itself as the highest wisdom and the most radiant beauty which our dull faculties can comprehend only in their primitive forms-this knowledge, this feeling is at the center of true religiousness."[1]

Man's Best Friend

Most of us have either heard or read about "man's best friend" or the dog traveling over great geographical distances and overcoming great physical hardships to be reunited with their master or mistress. Some dogs have even been reported to stand guard over the lifeless body of their owner, or be so bereaved at the death of an owner they keep a silent vigil at their master's grave, seemingly waiting for their return.

With this in mind, let's travel back to the year 1944 to a section of Norwood Road in West Hempfield Township. This road runs behind the mansion of the late Lloyd Mifflin, nineteenth century artist and poet, and one of Columbia's most famous former residents.

The rear of Mifflin's property had a tall fence which ran parallel to and along Norwood Road. The fence had a small wooden gate for the foot traveler, and a large entrance gate for horses and carriages. This particular stretch of road which lays to the rear of the mansion has been a hot spot for supernatural occurrences.

On a cold, crisp Autumn night in that year, a local fifteen year old boy was witness to an extraordinary happening. A responsible young man, one of his chores was to go for coal-oil, his trip taking him up the Norwood Road.

That particular night the moon was full and the country side was bathed in a soft glow. The young man, with no need for a light, carried his coal-oil can in one hand and rode his bicycle on his regular journey.

Returning, he coasted down the hill approaching the old Mifflin place on his left. Suddenly he caught a glimpse of a large dog trotting out of the shadows of the lane that led through the woods to a neighbor's house, and was situated opposite the small gate leading into the Mifflin residence.

Being fond of dogs, he slowed his bike to a stop and called to the animal which he described as being large, wolf-like, similar in color to a German Sheperd, but having a very large, broad head, much like the bone structure of a Labrador Retriever.

Without hesitation the dog made a bee-line for the boy, stopped and sat at the young man's feet. Sensing the dog was friendly, the young man reached down with his hand to pat the canine head. Just as his hand was to touch its furry mark, it felt no warm resistance, but passed straight through the dog's head. Shocked, he drew his hand back through the animal's cranium touching nothing but thin air.

At that moment the dog, whether restless with his interrupted night stroll, or not satisfied with the boy's company, stood up and trotted off . . . passing through the front wheel of the bicycle, spokes and all!

The petrified young man, staring in disbelief, watched as the strange image disappeared through the closed wooden gate leading to the Mifflin house.

Recovering from his frozen state he furiously pedaled his bike to his relative's house located about fifty yards down the road. Pounding on the door, his aunt greeted a pale, shaken and perspiring young man who blurted out his strange tale.

This was the first time he encountered a ghostly apparition on that certain stretch of Norwood Road, but it wouldn't be the last . . . read on.

The 'haunted' stretch of Norwood Road. Lloyd Mifflin's former residence, "Norwood" on right. (Photo by author, 1993.)

Miss Mary Mifflin of Norwood

The death of Miss Mary Mifflin of Norwood in 1881 has always been shrouded in mystery. She shared the family estate located in rural Columbia with her bachelor brothers, John Houston, James de Veaux, Charles West and Lloyd, the famed artist and poet. Mary's first cousin, Martha Mifflin, also resided at the home. As one can imagine, life could be rather fast and furious in a household of bachelors who enjoyed a "devil-may-care" attitude and a privileged life unfettered by financial worries.

Her brother Lloyd, the artist and poet, was a sensitive soul. He often reached inward for spiritual inspiration to compose his sonnets. Mifflin says in his notes: "In order that the poet write well it is necessary he enter into a sort of clairvoyant state... The best work I have ever done has been under these conditions."[1] One then wonders if he had any notion of the tragedy that was to befall his family.

On February 24, 1881 his beloved sister Mary was found dead in the house at Norwood; the exact cause of death was a bullet to the brain. How it happened was and is a matter for speculation. *The Lancaster Daily* Thursday, February 24, 1881 edition reads: "... it appears that Miss Mifflin was engaged in arranging the pillows on her father's bed when a revolver, which was lying under one of the pillows, was discharged from being disarranged, or while the unfortunate lady was in the set of removing it... The wildest stories are afloat this morning, but we believe the above to be the true version of the affair."

The other version is also given in the same article: "... Miss Mifflin started from the kitchen to the parlor to get some muslin for use in the tobacco shed. The report of the discharge of a firearm rang out . . . upon the servants rushing in she was found lying on her back on the floor dead, with a pistol lying on her bosom. It is supposed she picked the weapon up to remove it and it was accidently discharged."

The rendered verdict of the coroner's inquest was published in the *Lancaster New Era*, February 25, 1881 edition, ". . . came to her death by being shot in the head by the accidental discharge of a pistol which she was handling at the time." "The pistol was found lying on the floor near the body, from the position of which, it is evident, the fatal discharge took place while the deceased was in the act of placing the pistol in its accustomed place—a pigeon hole in the desk."

Whether Miss Mary was in her father's bedroom, fluffing pillows, or in the parlor, moving a gun to a pidgeon holed desk is uncertain. A clear senario has never been reported.

Publicly reported as an accident, it was the general understanding among the neighbors, (although only whispered in sincere deference to the well liked and respected Mifflin family) that Miss Mary took her own life. Her extreme distress, it was rumored, may have been caused by a social and moral indescretion commited by one of her brothers. Miss Mary was caught in the very center of staid and conservative Victorian American "blue-bloods" where etiquette and behavior followed unbendable rules. A severe breech of these rules by one of her own family was possibly more than she could bear.

Esther Helwig Hilgert (my great aunt) worked for the Mifflins in the early part of this century, doing various household chores. Esther Hilgert, though not born at the time of Mary's death, recalls her mother and aunt speaking of the funeral:

". . . My aunt Annie Campbell was a neighbor with the Mifflins, and she was the dressmaker. She made the dress for Miss Mary when she died . . . the dress that she was laid out in. It was a flowing grey silk dress. She (Miss Mary) had lovely red hair, and she was a beautiful person . . . tragic, tragic death. . ."

The beautiful, red haired young woman, beloved daughter and sister, laid in state in the west parlor of the Norwood home, as was the custom in those days. She was laid to rest at Mount Bethel Cemetery in Columbia . . . or was she truly at rest?

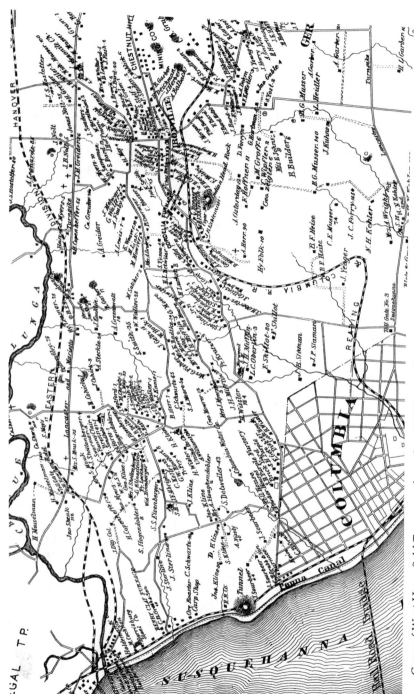

Copy of West Hempfield Twp. map from the 1875 Historical Atlas of Lancaster County Pennsylvania (Everts & Stewart).

Several months after his unforgettable experience of seeing the ghostly dog in 1944, the young man from Norwood started out on a late rainy afternoon on foot, carrying an umbrella. Spirit dogs or no spirit dogs, the coal-oil still was needed, but the boy started making his trips before the sun went down.

When he was just about at the large carriage gate of the Mifflin mansion, he glanced up from under his black umbrella, and saw a woman in a long, white, dress standing in the center of Norwood Road about thirty feet in front of him.

His first thought was, who was she, because he didn't recognize her. Most unusual, everyone knew everyone in this rural community, if only to say hello. He also wondered why she didn't have a coat, or an umbrella over the unusually long, floor length dress; for it was damp and cold and had been raining steadily all day.

Not breaking his stride, he got closer and greeted her with a "hello." The woman, who was facing him, slowly turned to her left, oblivious to him, and started to float (that's right . . . float!) across Norwood Road crossing in front of him. She disappeared as she floated through the small closed wooden gate, leading to the Mifflin place. Interesting enough, she was not wet from the rain, her dress softly billowing in the breeze.

The young man made record time to his relative's house. He did not go for coal-oil that day.

The relative who lived close by is now 87 years old. She remembers clearly the two occasions she comforted her nephew and remarked she had never again seen anyone so frightened.

Who was the woman who so silently traveled that spot of Norwood Road? Was it the spirit of Miss Mary Mifflin, the beautiful, red haired sister of Lloyd Mifflin who so tragically met her death in 1881?

And what about the ghostly dog who appeared to the same fifteen year old boy at the same place not many months before? Was the dog on an endless search for his master . . . or possibly his mistress?

Columbia's Haunted Museum

Visitors who tour the Columbia Historic Preservation Society's Museum may see more than just artifacts.

The museum, besides being the home of antiquities, old photos, and memorabilia of the town's past, also may be the home of a couple of very active ghosts.

The museum is located at 19–21 North Second Street in Columbia, Pa. Formerly a church erected in 1850; over the years its occupancy has changed.

Once the rafters rang with the sweet sounds of choirs and the grunts of nodding members of its congregation lulled into quiet sleep during sermons preached on hot summer Sundays, oblivious to their wives' rib-poking elbows.

In 1888 an adjoining parish house was built and occupied by the church minister. As time passed the minister and his family were housed elsewhere and the parish became the home of the church sexton.

The congregation, by 1952 had grown and moved to a new church at Fifth and Chestnut Street—the First English Lutheran Church. The buildings were sold and the Shaub machine shop took over the site. Its rafters then vibrated with the drone of machinery, and the beautiful hardwood floors became soaked with oil. Its aroma still permeating the air today.

By 1979, the machine shop had closed, and the fledging historical society acquired the site from the Columbia Area Improvement Authority.

According to Florence Miller, current President of the Society and her husband Bob, they have had several perplexing, if not hair-raising experiences at the site. Experiences they remember well.

Florence and Bob arrived at the society manse one day to do some work, when they heard noises coming from the second floor. It sounded as if some one was upstairs sorting through papers. Fearing an intruder had broken into the museum and found rare historical documents housed in various locations in the building, they investigated. The distinct sound of someone shuffling papers echoed through the hall but their investigation turned up a completely vacant building with nothing disturbed.

Another time, while working in the manse they were startled to hear the muffled voices of a man and woman talking as they descended the rear stairway. Florence said: "I knew it was a man and woman because I could hear their footsteps . . . one heavy, like a man, and the higher pitched clicks of a woman's heels on the stairs."

No one was there that time nor on the other separate occasions when they heard the pair stroll down the stairway in the front hallway.

Some time ago my husband Sam and I were helping host an "open house" museum tour. A lovely local lady, who as a girl attended church there, spoke of a kindly elderly couple who for many years lived in the manse and were caretakers of the property. She also spoke of a former minister and his wife and how devoted and committed they were to their congregation.

Could it be the spirits of one or more of those long since gone devoted people still remain at the former place of worship?

One spirit decided to get a bit physical with a society member, a sure way of getting one's attention. Edna Clark, museum historian, vividly recalled the day she and Mary Louise Miller were on the second floor going through old records.

Mrs. Clark was engrossed in some files when a cold, empty wind blew past her. In its passing she felt and heard the crack of a cold hand slap her firmly on the cheek. Shocked, dismayed and puzzled at Mary Louise's definitely unlady-like behavior, clutching her face she cried, "Why did you do that?"

The reply came from the adjoining room, "Did you say something Edna?"

Mrs. Clark inquired again: "Why did you slap me across the face?"

Mary Louise walked across the other room and peered through the doorway. She was now as puzzled as Mrs. Clark. Of course, she certainly didn't slap Edna. Not only was she not even in the same room as the victim, not a window in the whole place was open. Even the frigid, icy breeze could not be explained.

Mrs. Edna Clark was and is convinced she met a slap-happy ghost.

My husband and I have spent many hours at the society doing research work or helping with repairs and refurbishing. Once while I was alone at the Society searching through microfilm, I heard voices and footsteps coming from the front stairway area. This was strange for I had locked the front door behind me on entering.

About an hour after the incident Bob Miller arrived. I told him what I had heard.

With a little grin Bob asked, "Did you investigate to see who or what it was?"

I replied with no hesitation: "Of course not."

The Visitor

The events of the following story took place in Wrightsville, Pennsylvania located just across the Susquehanna River from the town of Columbia, in York County, Pennsylvania. It is not a ghost story or strange occurrence dealing with the supernatural. It is an unsolved mystery showing the inherent goodness in man, even men at war. It appears here in its entirety through the kind permission of author Gregory A. Coco who included it in his book, *On The Bloodstained Field II, 132 More Human Interest Stories of the Campaign and Battle Of Gettysburg* (Thomas Publications, Gettysburg, Pa. 1989).

Sunday, June 28, 1863, found lead elements of Lee's Confederate Army under General John B. Gordon, drawn up near Wrightsville, a small village on the east bank of the Susquehanna River. The town was defended by a Northern militia force commanded by Colonel Jacob Frick. During that day a short bombardment of the town and its defenses convinced Frick that his small command would be no match for Gordon's veteran troops. The village was abandoned and as soon as his men were safely over the river in Columbia, he destroyed the 5,620-foot, covered bridge. The Confederates entered Wrightsville and helped to extinguish the burning bridge that threatened the whole community. Gordon's men remained overnight, many billeting themselves in houses vacated by the citizens.

One of the homes so used was owned by the Samuel Smith family and was located on Locust Street across from the Methodist Church. The Smith's had a son named Silas who had joined the Union army earlier in the war. When he went off to fight, the family had given him a pocket testament inscribed with his name and home address on the flyleaf. Silas never returned to that home. He had been wounded, taken prisoner by the Rebels, and had died in a Southern hospital.

After the invaders had gone, the Smiths returned to their home to find Silas' testament on a table in one of the rooms which had been used by the Confederates. No message was left and nothing had been stolen or disturbed anywhere in the house.

Who left the boy's bible was never determined.

The Ironville Airship

Anyone who has ever seen a flying or hovering object in the sky, no matter how unlike aircraft of today it appears, will probably get the same, stock reply offered as an explanation from anyone who hears their story.

"Aw ... you probably saw an airplane." This rather broad explanation seems to satisfy the listener; but does little to clear the questions in the observer.

In 1975, a young, six year old Columbia boy saw something hovering above a meadow in Ironville. The meadow was situated on the corner where the Malleable Road intersects the Ironville Pike.

His excited astonishment at seeing the strange flying craft of course received the only "logical" adult explanation, "Aw ... you probably saw an airplane."

But today, 28 years later, he still vividly recalls his experience:

"... it was a large hat-shaped object which was hovering in the sky above the meadow. The "hat" had a rim and along the rim were little square window-shaped lights of different colors ... these were flashing on and off in sequence around the 'hat' rim."

He recalls watching it hover for a while, and then it shot off on an angle, up into the heavens and disappeared.

He's a grown man now and still hasn't been able to truly identify this craft. However he does know what it wasn't ... a twentieth century airplane.

The Legend of the Headless Horseman

The Ironville Pike still stretches through the hills surrounding Columbia town proper. Gently curving and following the lay of the land, it serves as a relatively straight route for those wishing to access Route 23, or the Old Marietta Pike, just west of the small village of Silver Spring, Pa.

Before the turn of the century, and as early as 1830, this area was a center of industry. The land, rich in iron ore, ochre, and silica sand was the site of several mining operations which employed many men. The small village of Ironville sprung up and the local Ironville Tavern was the gathering place for many workers after a long, hard day's work.

As legend has it, it was a night much like any other night in early Autumn. The tavern was hosting its regular customers, as they spun yarns, discussed the day's occupation and of course, downed countless mugs of lager. The walls of the hotel echoed with the good natured quips of her guests, who had not yet retired to their rooms or made the journey home. As the fireplace crackled and popped, one particular gentleman, already in a state of inebriation, ordered another drink for the road. He knew, all too well, the hours had slipped away again . . . unnoticed. He hoped the final drink would muffle the blow of the wrath of his "little woman" as he staggered through his kitchen door.

"I thought you had to be home by midnight?" asked one of his cohorts.

"That's right, midnight it is. My wife sleeps with the clock . . ." laughed the drunken husband.

"Well, its five minutes to twelve—you'll never make it into town by midnight," warned the friend.

Sheepishly, the wayward husband gulped his beer and slammed the heavy mug down on the table, announcing: "I'll be in Columbia by the stroke of midnight . . . or I'll be in Hell!"

Out the door he ambled, forcefully pushing his hat tighter over his head in preparation for the ride of his life. His horse seemed to sense his anxiety and danced in the dried leaves as his master mounted. The tipsey rider shouted to his friend watching from the tavern door. As his steed lurched into a gallop for home, his voice pierced the air: "Mark my words; I'll be in Columbia by midnight or I'll be in Hell!"

The cold air stung his eyes as he cut through the crisp, autumn air, urging his horse faster and faster. He reached the slight bend in the road, where it intersects Norwood Road. His horse, whether going too fast to make the bend or deciding (if a horse has problem solving capabilities) the shortest distance between two points is a straight line, thundered toward the low hanging branch of a tree.

The decapitated body of the rider was found the next day. His horse, who also had fallen, lay still, dead of a broken neck.

Many Ironville and Norwood residents, over the years claim to have heard the pounding hoof beats of a horse in the still of the night. Others, claim they've seen a horse with a headless rider, galloping along the Ironville Pike; and so a legend was born.

I had a strange experience many years ago which may be linked to this old legend. As a girl of 13, I was spending the night at my grandmother's home in Norwood. Her house was situated on the highest hill in that area. The lane to her property connected with Norwood Road several hundred feet north of the intersect of the Ironville Pike, where the horse and rider supposedly met their deaths.

I recall that evening vividly, for it was the first time in my short 13 years of life that I remained awake all night and greeted the dawn. Grandmother never spoke of ghosts or legends around us grandchildren because she never wished to cause us fear. But that cold autumn night, shortly after the clock reached 12 midnight, I heard the faint pounding of hoof beats.

They Swear By Ghost Yarn, And Columbian Knows It!

Shades of Ichabod Crane!

The yarn of the "Headless Horseman," as recounted in a feature story in last week's edition has had repercussions. Several letters have been received at this office from mail subscribers to the Broadcaster who live along the Ironville Pike stating "Positively" that they have, on numerous occasions, seen the beheaded spectre going galloping noiselessly along the highway toward his legendary Columbia Rendezvous.

But perhaps the most interested reader of the feature last week was Philip Glatfelter, who recalled an experience he had about a year ago which offered sufficient proof that Ironville folk aren't taking any chances with the ridin' ghost. Glatfelter, well known local scout leader, enjoys horseback riding, and an occasional moonlight canter through th surrounding country.

It was on one of these rides, as his mount trotted slowly home, that he was started to hear the resounding bang of a shotgun from a nearby farmyard. Before he could gather his wits, a second, third and fourth shot followed, all aimed in his general direction, and one load barely missing him. Having never heard of the legend, Glatfelter was at a loss to know what all the shooting was about, but he says he gathered the general idea that he was not very welcome in the neighborhood, and he spurred his steed into a gallop which lasted until he reached Columbia.

It was not until sometime later that the Columbian, through inquiry, was able to establish the theory that he was mistaken by a superstitious believer as the fearsome "Headless Horseman" of Ironville.

A newspaper article in files of author. Unfortunately, no exact date is mentioned. Story appeared in the "Broadcaster," a Columbia publication circulated between 1931 and 1943.

As the hours of the morning wore on, the sound grew louder and seemed to first come from the acreage behind her home. Then it seemed to be coming from the area where the Cloverton housing development is now situated. That area was an open field many years ago.

At first I thought it was the bass, rythmic pounding of a distant stereo, or someone pounding bongos or a drum. Then I thought it might be the sound of my own heart beating in my ears, for I was scared in my ignorance ... no, it wasn't that. On four different occasions that night, I climbed the stairs to awaken my grandmother and pleaded with her to listen at the window. I hoped she could explain just what I was hearing. She sleepily got out of bed and told me she heard nothing, it was my imagination, and that I was to go back to bed.

I went back to bed, but I certainly didn't sleep; for that horse rode over the fields till the crack of dawn. It was only many years later that I heard of the legend of the headless horseman. Was this the explanation for my sleepless night?

The Ironville Tavern still stands disguised in its twentieth century aluminum siding trappings. The unfortunate horseman's name has been lost to the ages, but his spirit may still linger on, forever doomed to repeat . . . the ride of his life.

Mystery Blast and Falling Ice

The summer of 1957 greeted Columbia residents with a "boom" ... literally. Town residents and people living as far away as Wissler's Hill frequently felt and heard the percussion of the blasting done by the Pennsylvania Department of Transportation[1] as they chiseled a trough through Chickies Rock to connect Columbia and Marietta by road (Route 441).

State engineers on the job site said:

> "... (the cut) was a remarkable feat and one seldom equalled in the history of road building in Pa."[2]

At 8 P.M. on Tuesday, July 30, 1957 a blast rocked Columbia which shook homes, rattled dishes and window panes and was felt as far north as Selinsgrove. About a year before this episode, a similar blast was felt extending from below Holtwood as far as Middletown and as far east as Elizabethtown and Mt. Joy.[3]

Columbians paid little attention to the blast and most thought it was just another dynamite charge, another rather powerful one set off during the Chickies Road work.

However, state officials said no blasting was going on at this time. Also, officials at the Olmsted Air Force Depot at Middletown discounted the theory of a jet breaking the sound barrier.[4]

A stranger curiosity is that at the same time as Columbians were feeling and hearing the blast, a farmer working in his fields at Bernville, a small town five miles north of Reading, narrowly escaped serious injury or death by falling ice.

Three fifty pound chunks of ice dropped from over head and narrowly missed him. The ice penetrated the ground at his feet

. . . and if you think this is strange, remember it happened in the dead of summer!

Pennsylvania State Troopers Phillip Melley and Richard Fisher confirmed the ice was real but could give no adequate explaination,[5] other than it was ice; and it did fall out of the heavens.

What are the odds of getting beaned on the head by a celestial brickbat? Very slim . . . but tell that to Ann Elizabeth Hodges. On November 30, 1954, the then 32 year old woman was snoozing on her living room couch in Sylacauga, Alabama. She was narrowly missed by a blackened rock the size of a bowling ball which crashed through her roof and landed on the living room floor.

The rock was a meteorite. Mrs. Hodges, who died in 1972 (of other causes) holds the distinction of being the only confirmed human actually to be struck by a falling extraterrestrial body. (A dog, however, was killed by a three-pound meteorite that fell on Egypt in 1911.)[6]

Mrs. Hodges beat the odds of one in 17 billion. Near misses don't count. In an average year, half a dozen small meteorites strike the Earth close enough to human observers to be recovered.[7]

Meteorites are not the only things floating around out in space. Maybe the odds of getting hit by a piece of man-made, earth orbiting trash are less. More than 3,300 tons of junk—everything from derelict satellites and used rockets to flecks of paint and shreds of tile—whiz around Earth at speeds averaging 20,000 miles an hour.[8]

Our space walking astronauts have a very hazardous job. John Pike, a scientist and watchdog of the space agency says: "One of the risks of doing a spacewalk is that somebody's ham sandwich from 20 years ago is going to hit you." At that velocity even a marble size piece of junk would hit with the force of an office safe falling 100 feet to the ground.[9]

Yes, it's getting crowded up there. Current shuttle blastoff missions not only look for "weather windows" but the June, 1993 *Endeavour* mission had to look for a "garbage gap."

Maybe the strange blast and falling ice in 1957 was a really strange occurence then. But 50 years from now? . . . maybe not.

An Eerie Old House in New Texas

Mrs. Bette Atkinson and her husband got more than they bargained for when they bought a house in New Texas in August of 1975. The small village is located south of Peach Bottom in southern Lancaster County. A scenic rural area, Mrs. Atkinson, her husband and 15 year old son expected a quiet home . . . but that was wistful thinking.

Faceless voices, hysterical laughter, footsteps coming up the stairs when she and her husband were the only two people in the house, and in sight of each other, were the unexpected "extras" that came with the house.

Not frightened off, the family lived there for two years, having rented out their adjacent mobile home. Her first encounter occurred in September of 1975. The following is her account:

"I had gone over to clean the windows because they were so dirty you couldn't see out of them. I used all the window cleaner so my husband and son went over to Rock Springs Store to buy more. I bent over to pick up the polishing cloth to finish the window when a voice asked me, 'What are you doing?'. I answered, turning around, fully expecting to see my husband's uncle standing there. But no one was there! My husband and son returned shortly and I told them of my experience. They were as puzzled as I."

They moved into the house a few months later. Returning home after a short trip, the three Atkinsons were in the kitchen fixing dinner, when they heard someone walk up the stairs and across the bedroom floor above them. No one was there!

They soon discovered something was "rotten in Denmark".

While moving boxes upstairs for storage, they opened the attic door. According to Bette Atkinson, "The stench was enough to make us gag."

Putting the boxes down they went downstairs for another load. Returning they found that the odor was gone from the attic. Relieved, they trekked back down the stairs only to find the stench was now in the kitchen.

"It smelled like something was dead for a week", said Bette Atkinson.

Mrs. Atkinson recalled the night she was awakened from her sleep for no apparent reason. Clearing her eyes, she saw a yellow glow along the opposite wall and ceiling. She recalled:

"Within that glow was the most beautiful old time children's carousel with shimmering lavender, blue and pink zoo animals twirling in the light. I watched, dumbfounded, until it gradually faded away. It was the most beautiful thing I ever saw but I was too stunned even to wake my husband."

She tried to convince herself she was dreaming, but a few weeks later she mentioned it to her mother-in-law. Much to the surprise of both of them, her mother-in-law said she had the exact same experience in the same room while an overnight guest just a month prior.

Eventually, the Atkinsons converted the house into two apartments. They rented the one apartment to two young ladies recently discharged from the U.S. Navy. Purposely Mrs. Atkinson neglected to tell them about any of the unusual occurrences in the house. Thinking it best not to alarm them, she thought they should draw their own conclusions if anything unusual happened.

Sure enough, one night one of the young women came to her door and asked her assistance. She needed help to find the baby who's cries echoed in the house.

This was one experience Mrs. Atkinson never had while she lived there. But a woman who occupied the house in the early 1950's later told Mrs. Atkinson that she often had heard the crying infant in the house.

The two female tenants also told of some one talking to them, calling them by name but no one being there. The young women eventually moved out, going their separate ways.

The Atkinsons decided to get a new mobile home and so moved back into one of the apartments until their new home was set up. Well, "IT" was back to the same tricks again. She would hear noises as if someone was moving heavy furniture. The noise would go on for nearly an hour . . . then dead silence! Bette Atkinson sums up her sentiments about the old place:

"At times the hairs on the back of my neck would stand on end. . . . I still live next door to the house but no longer own it. Other tenants of the house have heard odd things. Some have moved out after only several months and some stay a little longer. In a way, I would like to know what had caused these strange happenings. But again, something tells me I am better off not knowing."[1]

Pennsylvania Witch Trial

The Pennsylvania judicial record lists only one instance of a prosecution for witchcraft.[1] In 1683, Margaret Matson and Yeshro Hendrickson (of Swedish descent) were accused of being witches and found guilty.

William Penn sat in judgement. Lacy Cock acted as interpreter. Absentee jury men were fined 40 shillings each.[2]

The following is a sample of the evidence presented:

"Henry Dryistreett, attested, saith he was told 20 years ago, that the witness at the bar was a witch, and that several cows were bewitched by her." "Annaky Coolin, attested, saith that her husband took the heart of a calf that had died, as they thought, by witchcraft and boiled it, whereupon the prisoner at the bar came in and asked them what they were doing; they said boiling of flesh; she said they had better they had boiled the bones, with several other unseemly expressions."

Even Margaret Matson's daughter testified against her, but "the prisoner denieth all things".[3]

Governor William Penn charged the jury, which brought in an ambiguous and ineffective verdict for such a dubious offense. They found her "guilty of the common fame of being a witch, but not guilty in manner and form as she stands indicted." The women were released and put on their good behavior for six months.[4]

The Goat

A young Columbia couple, armed with a camera, set out on a brisk February afternoon hike. Their sunny afternoon stroll was a pleasant break from several days of winter rain and they headed for the little quarry situated south of Manor Street and behind the Columbia airport.

Knowing the area, they headed down the wall of the quarry to where a chiseled out section of rock formed a very shallow cave. The young woman reached the cave first and squatted under the protective walls of the rock while she waited for her camera wielding husband to descend the narrow path.

Suddenly, several rocks bounced down the slope and the young woman quietly peered out hoping to see a raccoon, fox or some other woodland creature. Much to her surprise, standing on the ledge above was a long-haired goat with unusually long, gracefull horns . . . staring back at her. She quickly scanned the hill hoping to get her husband's attention; possibly he could get a picture of the unexpected creature.

There was her husband; half-way down the hill, smiling and waving, looking up in the direction of the goat. She asked him if he got the picture of the goat.

Puzzled, he replied, "Goat . . . what goat? I was waving at three people up on that ledge . . . see?" When he looked back again they were gone.

Climbing back up the hill to investigate just who saw what, they reached the ledge above the cave. The soft, wet earth showed no trace that something had tread there . . . animal or human. Her husband who had been too busy waving a greeting to the people he saw, never took a picture.

The Haunted Mill House

Along the banks of the Conestoga River, on the outskirts of Millersville, stands a nineteenth century mill house. Situated at the end of a dead-end road, the mill is removed from the hustle and bustle of traffic. A rather quiet place, it was home to a young married couple, Greg and Karen D. Mrs. D. sent me a written account of a series of strange occurrences that happened to her in the house. These events, Karen thinks, were caused by the spirit of a young child, in ghost terms referred to as a poltergeist.

According to Karen, "things" began to happen around the time she and her husband started to discuss plans to move to another area.

It was March of 1992, around 9 PM. Karen, a full-time college student at Millersville University, was sitting on the floor in the living room working on a school project. Her husband was upstairs sleeping, the family cat balled up at his feet. Sitting amid her array of school materials, her body was facing the television so she could grab a glance at the screen every now and then.

"I felt something push my right shoulder as if trying to get my attention," wrote Karen.

She quickly turned around fully expecting to see what her husband or her cat wanted. Nothing was there.

Karen continued: "For a few minutes I had myself convinced that I felt not a thing. Then suddenly I felt a push on my right thigh as I was (now) lying on my left side watching TV. Once again, I turned around and absolutely nothing was there. This time I knew that I had experienced something, but was not sure what it was. To be quite honest, I was quite perturbed at the thing which was 'picking' on me so I said aloud, 'Whatever or whoever you are, please leave me alone; I am trying to work!' That was the last I felt of the pushes."

Badly frightened, and the fact that Karen's husband worked third shift, she spent the next several weeks sleeping on the downstairs sofa. Finally she summoned enough courage to spend the night alone in their own bed.

At 6 AM she was rudely awakened by five incredible, loud BOOMS!! She sat bolt upright, swung her legs out over the bed, stood up and reached for the rifle and shells. Calmly and quietly she telephoned her parents. They suggested she check for footprints in the freshly fallen snow . . . no footprints. The joint decision was made that she make her way downstairs to the extension telephone fully prepared to shoot anything that moved along the way. When she got to the stairway, she was greeted by their cat who had transformed into a giant fur-ball, and seemed as frighted as she was. Safely reaching the telephone in the kitchen, and finding no intruder, she called her mother back with the news. That was the last night she slept upstairs alone for a while.

Months passed. Karen became weary of the couch and courageously returned to her own bed. At 2 AM that morning she was awakened by a LOUD beep, beep, beep sound. Some how the clock radio in the bathroom across the hall had turned on but the regular 24 hour country music station that it was always tuned to was not to be heard. Thinking her husband had left it on, she turned it off and went back to bed. The next day she was surprised to hear that her husband wasn't responsible for her brief awakening. He had used the downstairs bathroom the evening before.

It was back to the downstairs couch for Karen. Shortly after retiring, the beep, beep, beep noise began again. Karen said: "This time I knew that my husband did not use the bathroom before going to work, and how in the world did that clock radio turn itself on? Needless to say, I was quite afraid, however, I had to go and turn the radio off for it was that loud I couldn't have possibly slept. This time I unplugged it and packed it away in a box the next morning. I could not come up with any possible explanation as to what I experienced and neither could anyone else!"

According to Karen, there are other "wierd" events that took place in the house for which she had no explanation. Strange flashing and dancing lights appeared to race through the spare bedroom which adjoined their bedroom. These lights couldn't be explained for the house was situated at the end of a dead end road. There was no traffic nor was there a dusk to dawn light on the property.

Karen summed up her thoughts about the noisy activity: "Later on I found out that there once was a little girl who died in the house around the turn of the century. Her remains were found by the builders who were constructing an addition onto the mill house. It is my opinion that it was the little girl who was doing different things to me, but in a playful manner. Before we left the house in July of 1992 I told her what we were doing (moving to another residence). (Although I fully expected something more to happen) no incidents took place after that. . . ."

The Girls of Kinderhook

Lancaster County is dotted with tiny villages, many of which do not appear on any map. Local inhabitants are aware of their existence even if some discussion may be needed to actually pin down exact boundaries. One such village is known as Kinderhook.

Travelers seeking the quiet little area need only follow Kinderhook Road from where it intersects the Ironville Pike in Columbia, Pennsylvania. In 1883, Franklin Ellis described the village of Kinderhook as "... containing two or three dozen houses, scattered over Chestnut Hill on the public road leading from Columbia to the Marietta and Lancaster turnpike.[1]

The village name was coined during the midst of the 1840 political campaign when Dr. George Kline, an ardent supporter of Martin Van Buren and the sage of Kinderhook, named the hamlet in Van Buren's honor; for Van Buren was born in Kinderhook, New York.[2] It seems as if Dr. Kline was the only Democrat in the neighborhood and the Whigs and Republicans tried for many years to have the name changed but, as is evidenced, these attempts were in vain. The name remains today, as well as the two or three dozen houses (with few additions) as was described in the mid-nineteenth century.[3]

One of the still standing houses is our house, or should I say my great great grandfather Kappler's house. It still occupies the original parcel of land it was built on in 1868 (however, not the *exact* spot, for great great grandpap Kappler moved structures for a living and relocated the house closer to Kinderhook Road before the turn of the century). Most local folks know it as "The Old Smith Place", but few survive who remember it as the location of a thriving blacksmith business. Here great grandfather Henry Dietz Smith shod horses and the dangerous and ornery mule, along with making wagon wheels and tobacco shears.

Oddly enough, the house has never been lived in or owned by anyone but family . . . and sometimes I think some of the previous four generations haven't left. I'll tell you why . . .

Maude Kappler Smith Robb was the last inhabitant of the house before my husband and I moved there. Aunt Maude was born there, as well as her sisters Martha, Pauline and Eleanor (Elo for short), and brothers Harry and Salem. The brothers married (Salem eventually became my grandfather). Maude, however, was the only daughter to marry, making her home in Florida.

By 1953, the three single sisters were the sole occupants of the home. Martha and Pauline were beauticians. Their shop, located for 30 years in the old Steven's House hotel in Lancaster, flourished. Elo, the 4' 10" domestic dynamo, took care of the house.

All three sisters shared a deep love for their home. It was filled with golden memories of childhood . . . the only home they ever knew or even cared to know. A private Shangra-La, where changes were made only by pre-supposing postmortem wishes of long gone family members. An idyllic setting, unscathed by change.

Change struck an ugly blow in 1976. Sister Martha, best friend, business partner, head of household, and family decision maker suddenly died. Her passing had a devastating effect on her sisters.

Pauline plunged into a state of melancholia. Attempts by sister Elo, and other family members to comfort her, were in vain. Pauline's behavior at times was rather bizarre . . . refusing to even make the bed in which her sister died. Eventually the covers were straightened, but everything in the room remained untouched as if waiting for the owner's return.

My grandmother, Leanora Helwig Smith, worried greatly about her surviving sister-in-laws. A wise and kind-hearted woman, she often said that the living must not mourn the dead indefinitely or un-relentingly. When one does, the soul of the departed cannot find peace. It lingers, torn between this world

Aunts Elo, Pauline, Martha and Maude pose on the front porch of their ancestral folk Victorian home at Kinderhook, PA., circa 1910.

and the other. I believe that to be true for a strange thing happened one day during a visit with my aunts.

It was almost a year since Martha's death when Aunt Pauline, Aunt Elo and I sat in the dining room of the home at Kinderhook, discussing various topics. My attention was suddenly diverted to creaking hardwood floors over head. A pall fell over the conversation as we listened to the slow and deliberate footsteps of someone walking the entire length of the second floor. The sound passed directly over our heads stopping directly over the kitchen area.

I asked the girls if they had company- other than me of course. My aunts, quickly exchanged glances and in unison they said: "No."

"Then who is walking around upstairs?" I inquired.

"Did you hear anything, Elo?" asked Aunt Pauline.

Aunt Elo replied, "Why . . . no . . . did you hear any . . ."

Her reply was interrupted by footsteps deliberately making their return trip through the upstairs bedroom.

"Those footsteps!" I said.

"Oh." replied my aunts.

"Now ladies . . ." I said with a smile. ". . . I know I have not lost my mind, and those are footsteps as opposed to any other noise I could compare it with."

"Oh, those noises . . . we hear that every now and then. Just house noises. We don't have company."

Sure enough, there wasn't another living soul in the house besides us three. But that experience came in handy when many years later, Aunt Maude told me about her sleepless nights. . . .

Aunt Maude looked at me through pale, blue eyes stung with tears of grief. "They came again last night, like they do every night, Dottie. I'm only telling you, because you won't think I'm crazy. You don't think I'm crazy . . . do you?"

No, Aunt Maude wasn't crazy. But it was possible the terrible strain of losing the only remaining members of her family, her sisters Pauline and Elo, within three weeks was more than the 89 year old widow could bear. She had travelled by train from Miami the previous year to help sister Pauline care for Elo, who was in failing health.

Without warning, Pauline died suddenly. Elo followed shortly therafter.

I asked her if she knew where her sisters were. She answered: "Of course, they're dead; all of them. But they still come every night. Just about the time I start to fall asleep or sometimes after I've dozed off, I hear Pauline call my name. And she's persistent, she keeps calling until I sit up . . . and then I see her."

Maud described her sister Pauline as wearing a pale blue dress, of sheer, delicate fabric. Transparent in appearance, almost glowing, she would glide out of the adjoining bedroom, stopping and staring at the rudely awakened sleeper.

Beseechingly, the apparition would stretch out her arm and beckon the only living occupant of the room to join her. After receiving no reply, (Aunt Maude refused to speak to her) the ghost would glide past the bed and into the rear bedroom.

According to Aunt Maude, sometimes the whole gang showed up. That is, Pauline was accompanied by her other deceased sisters, Martha and Elo.

Aunt Maude's biggest complaint about the ghostly visits was not that she was terribly frightened, but that it was impossible to sleep at night. Aunt Maude complained: "They want me to come with them. Constantly calling me ... I may be old Dottie, but it's not my time to go. Only God decides that, not me, not the 'girls'. . . . I believe there is a reason I am the only one left. It's a terrible thing to be the only survivor, very lonely, but I'm not going till I'm supposed to (go) ... there is a reason."

Great Aunt Maude Kappler Smith Robb was called (by God) for the last time in 1990 at the age of 94.

Our family now occupies that pink house in Kinderhook. I often smell permanent wave solution, or the fragrance I associate with my aunt Maude.

One day while cleaning the dining room I backed into someone, forcing me to instinctively say: "Excuse me." ... no one was there. Puzzled, I continued my cleaning, when I felt a hand push me on the shoulder so forcefully, I dropped my cleaning rag. Of course, no one was there.

My husband Sam was sleeping late one morning when his attention was captured by the sound of the hardwood floors squeaking. As he opened his eyes he saw "me" sitting on the dresser which is along side of our bed. Dressed in "my" robe, I nimbly jumped off, floorboards squeaking with the landing. Walking past him and around the foot of the bed I disappeared into the adjoining bedroom (formerly Aunt Martha's). He talked to me and receiving no reply, nor hearing any more movement, he went to investigate. The room was totally empty of any human life form. His search for me ended downstairs in the kitchen, where I had been for the past hour.

Sometimes our sons see the transparent visage of one of the girls standing at the foot of their beds. Ocassionally, one will float across one of the upstairs bedrooms. The apparitions only make themselves visible to the male occupants of the house, which is everyone but me. Go figure ... that's just like a woman.

I have often wondered why Aunt Maude was the only survivor. She was convinced there was a reason, but just how her survival figured in the grand scheme of life may never be fully understood. I, however, feel very fortunate to have gotten to know her. She, as well as her sisters, were four of the most interesting women I have ever known.

Some may have viewed them as eccentric. Maybe, but they were smart, witty, kind and sentimental. Hard working women

"THE OLD SMITH PLACE" has changed little since 1868. It has been in the same family for five generations. (photo by Bob Miller.)

who made it in the days when it was definitely a man's world, successfully running a thriving business for 38 years.

They never gossiped, and guarded their privacy with a vengeance. Many may have felt excluded from their lives but I was embraced. For that, they have always made me feel special. I thank them.

Yes, I do miss them. But not as much as one might think. You see, they still live here.

Chicques Hill Haunting

The rolling farmland of Lancaster County bares its bone in a precipitous cliff at Chicques along the Susquehanna River. The craggy rock summit, located a mile and a half above (north west of) Columbia, Pennsylvania, has felt the muffled tread of moccasined Indian feet. Shawanese and Susquehannocks were two of the Indian tribes described by John Wright, believed to be the first white man to feast his eyes on the Susquehanna Valley near Columbia in 1724.[1] One can only imagine the men behind the eyes that have enjoyed the breath-taking view of the river valley over the centuries.

By 1893, the Chicques Hill area was enjoyed by hundreds who frequented a park established there. Located a safe distance east of the sheer rock cliff, the park had a restaurant, dancing pavilion and picnic tables. There, young couples enjoyed the moonlit evenings; romance had its beginning and sometimes its end in the same place where generations of the Redman had roamed the forest.

Chicques has always had a long history of alleged hauntings. Shortly before the turn of the century, the area was supposed to have been "cursed" by a disgruntled, aged woman. Several sources I contacted stated tradition holds that she was a witch. When evicted from her home which was situated on Chicques Hill, she retaliated by "cursing" the area making it unfit for all others to occupy.[2]

In August, 1969, a wild rumor spread throughout Columbia and surrounding areas. Several local youths who had been at Chicques Hill the week of August 20th claimed they had seen a "ghost". Word got around. During the week of the full moon of August 24, 1969, crowds gathered nightly at the entrance of the road that led to the old Chicques Park. Fearing accidents or a massive traffic jam, even the Columbia, West Hempfield, and East Donegal police were on the scene.[3]

An estimated two hundred people were at the park entrance on Tuesday, August 26, 1969. It was reported in the *Columbia News* that about one half of the crowd saw the ghost that evening. They described it as:

".... (a) large, formless and of a misty greyish-silver appearance.... Oddly enough, those who claim they saw the spectre moving through the woods well above ground level furnished identical descriptions."[4]

These daily ghost vigils continued to draw crowds. The assembly on Wednesday, August 27, 1969 approached 500 in number. However, the ghost was a "no-show". The local news said the crowd was not disappointed:

"... They saw in its absence confirmation of their contention that its appearance could not be attributed to either moonlight or auto headlights casting weird shadows among the trees. Nor, they said, could its appearance be attributed to the 'madness' which affects so many people when the moon approaches its full stage. Many were confident the ghost would make its appearance again."[5]

Hundreds said they saw this apparition during that week in 1969 but the initial "sighting" was officially disclaimed to be a hoax. "Penitent Youths Confess to Hoax" read the headline in the *Columbia, Pa., News*, August 29, 1969 edition. The teenagers who started the rumor were reported to have been under the influence of "sneaky Pete", a modestly priced (cheap) grade of wine. They decided to "raise a ghost" and pass the story on, never realizing it would grow to such enormous proportions among the locals.[6]

A more bazaar incident happened in 1946. The local newspaper referred to this earlier sighting in its coverage of the "hoax haunting". This prompted a letter to the editor of the newspaper from Columbia resident, Mrs. Harriet Horn. Her letter was written "to set the record straight", for she and her friends were the ones who saw a beastly apparition at Chicques Hill twenty years before. The letter appeared in the *Columbia, Pa., News*,

Chickies Park concession stand, favorite picnicing area of local residents. Photo taken c. 1900. Courtesy of Bob Miller.

Friday, August 29, 1969 edition. She describes her experience in her own words. I have included it here in its entirety:

To The Ghost Hunters of Columbia:

This is an open letter to the public to correct a few errors which were made in Thursday's Columbia News. Perhaps the writer was a bit shook up when it was printed. I am the woman who has had an experience at Chickies Hill, in 1946 and not 1944. I do not exactly believe in ghosts but I know what I saw with my own eyes and you know, seeing is believing. I wish to relay the exact story as it took place, at that time. It seems simple enough to talk about it now, but was not so, at that time. I had to watch who ever I would tell it to over the years for fear, of you know what. I remained quiet about the experience for quite awhile, before I had the nerve to talk about it. However since others have seen this so called apparition, I feel, I'm glad I wasn't the only one to see it and that I don't doubt anyone of them. To me it was no dream of any sort, for I have remembered it many years and not as a pleasant memory.

First of all, I am from the east end of town, not the north end.

It was like this, I worked for Wyeth Inc., at the time and I was 18 years of age. We, in a certain department decided to hold a picnic at Chickies.

We went there before dark and sat things up, back in off the road to the left, going toward Marietta. We weren't there long and it was suggested that a certain fellow (from Marietta), and I, go to the pump for water. We got in the car and about a half block down the dirt road, on the way out, all of a sudden, on the right side of the road (in Chickies) I, or we saw a gigantic figure of at least 16 ft. or more (narrow) about 1 ft. and ½ wide, flat against one of the real tall trees. I looked and saw, no feet or arms, only straight up that high, and at the top there was a head of bandages, like a mummie, with six knives, three on each side of the head. We were so scared, he could hardly drive the car onto the main road which was a couple of feet away. He kept saying "My God what is it (?)".

We reached the main road in shock, we drove about ¼ mile or so and stopped dead and just sat; looking and wondering.

Then I said, "Forget the water! we gotta go back in there and tell the rest to get out!" We were so scared we figured we'd go in real fast and we scuffed up the dirt. We got out of the car and with just a look at us and saying, "You gotta get out of here, we saw something terrible!". In a moment things were thrown and all left, real fast like.

We never did have the picnic.

The next day at work all was silent and only one woman who was much older than I told me the story about the old lady, that lived there and what had happened to her.

I was frightened about the place, even after that. Even today, I dread going past in a car.

I can not speak for what others have seen, only for myself and this is the truth. As the paper stated other things I have told, which are also a fact, not fiction.

However, I would strongly advise anyone not to go there with the idea of thinking its fun, because its not.

It may be to ones sorrow, so, stay away if you know what is best, or good for you, take it from me.

I'm sure the fellow from Marietta a few years ago, that ran out of the same place on to the road and stopped (my) brother (in fright and shock) and ask(ed) him, to take him "in the name of God" to Marietta, that he just seen something terrible(!) (He) will tell you the same as I am telling you. All to stay away.

I feel if there is one person so brave to defy the unknown or, whatever, it would not be wise.

There (is) a reason for all this and perhaps it leads back to Indian times. Who is to say.

If you remember when the new road to Marietta was being put through, the Columbia paper had a picture of a huge bolder in the middle of the road, which there was no answer to how, who or what put it there. Look it up and you'll see this is correct. Well I could say a lot more but I don't wish to take up all the paper, as, I can write like mad when I get started.

I thank the editor for letting me tell you my story and its not for bed time.

Good night and everyone have pleasant dreams (of ghosts).

I remain, a sane citizen of your town (and) mine,

Mrs. Harriet Horn

Mrs. Horn's graphic description of the demon she saw in 1946 was very similar to what one person saw when he gathered with 200 other people on August 26, 1969.

> ". . . instead (of him describing a mummified head emerging at the top of a black shroud) he said it appeared to him as a head that was wrapped in bandages and that one knife protruded through the bandage."[6]

Mrs. Horn, in her letter to the editor, spoke of a large boulder which was found in the center of the roadway while Route 441 was under construction. I tried to find more information on this curiosity. Unfortunately, I came up with no supporting evidence. This does not mean that Harriet Horn is incorrect . . . it just means I haven't found the newspaper article. Searching through microfilm can be very tedious work; an ill-timed sneeze, or a long blink, and the researcher can whiz right by an article. I will continue searching, maybe I will still have success.

The ghost at Chicques is very interesting indeed. John C. Musser, staff writer for *The Columbia News* in his coverage of the 1969 sightings summed it up perfectly:

> "Ghost or no ghost, however, a legend has been established in the past week (August 24-30, 1969) adding another specter to the already ghost ridden Columbia area.
> And, its a foredrawn conclusion in years to come, some of these youngsters who saw the ghostly visitor will relate the story to their children who in turn will pass it down to theirs."[7]

Lane Leading Back to Chiques' Park. c. 1940. Photo courtesy of Bob Miller.

Shank's Tavern in Marietta

Shank's Tavern, built 1814, as it appears today. (Photo courtesy Bob Shank and Ephrata Science Press.)

Along the streets of the little Susquehanna River town of Marietta stand buildings which sheltered souls of a by-gone era. One such building, if walls could speak, could weave a fascinating tale. Built in 1814, Shank's Tavern is located on the corner of Front and Waterford Streets. It has been in continuous operation as a tavern since James Madison served as the fourth president of the United States, only closing for a short time during the flood of 1972.

In the early nineteenth century, when the tavern opened its doors to the public, Marietta was a "boom" town. A bustling inland port, the community had a busy canal system, which eventually gave way to railroads, iron furnaces, and of course, the multitude of people needed as workers.

The Shank family has owned the tavern since 1930. Robert Shank, Jr., the current owner, recently extended his gracious hospitality and gave the author and her husband a first-hand account of his experiences and a tour of the quaint tavern.

As one crosses the threshold of the stately building, his feet tread on the name "Maullic" spelled out in blue and white mosaic tile. This former owner was also a Marietta beer brewer in the nineteenth century. He is responsible for the rear elevation three story addition to the tavern.

Mr. Shank, the current owner, has no knowledge of any tragic events happening in the tavern over the centuries. The ghostly inhabitants of the old hotel therefore cannot be explained by a violent death which paraphycologists say often go hand in hand with a haunting. He spoke of the Fritz brothers who owned the tavern in the 1800's, prior to Maullic. It was rumored there was a great deal of sibling rivalry and jealousy between the two. One of the brothers didn't trust in the banking system. When he passed away, no one was able to find any of his money and many speculated that he buried or stashed it somewhere in the tavern.

Bob Shank, while digging in the cellar after the 1972 flood, felt his shovel strike a hard object.

"I thought I had just found the 'Mother-load'," smiled Shank.

His back-breaking labor, however, didn't uncover a hidden stash of gold. A perfectly preserved 40 gallon earthenware crock was his reward. Mr. Shank thinks it may have been placed in the low spot of the dirt floor cellar as a catch basin in the century past. It still occupies a place of honor, close to where it laid buried for decades.

Mr. Shank spoke about the tavern during the early canal and railroad days:

> "There have been a lot of humans and souls and whatever pass through this place since 1814. . . . Front Street was a 'seedy' section of town (in the early 1800's) . . . shady characters and people boozin' it up. This used to be a hotel also. They'd rent rooms for a quarter a night and some of the rooms were nicer than the others.

Some of them (rooms) you had to 'flop' in and for a quarter you could just lay down."

Mr. Shank vividly recalls a strange event that happened to him and his brother many years ago:

"My brother and I grew up here; and when I was 15, he was some where around eleven (years old). Sunday nights was always real spooky in here because it was so quiet. Every night of the week you heard car doors, voices, juke box playing, . . . the cigarette machine, when they pulled it, hit the pipes and you could hear it upstairs where my brother and I would sleep.

To get up to where our bedroom was you had to come through this back door, which is always locked. So for anybody to be up there on a Sunday night, well,- nobody was living there but us- and everything was dead quiet.

(One night) we were laying on our bunk beds and all of a sudden . . . BAM! . . . BAM! . . . BAM!, something pounded on our bedroom door! I asked my brother, 'Did you hear that?' He said, 'Yeah!'.

I climbed out of my bunk and asked, 'Who is it?'. There was no answer. I looked under the bottom of the door (there is about an inch of clearance between the floor and the door) and there were no feet! I said, 'We better go get Mom!'.

Now, Mom lived in another apartment and she had to go down a couple of steps to get over to where we slept. We told her somebody was out there and she said, 'Now you know there is no way somebody could be out there . . . the doors are locked!'.

We went back to bed and in those days we had metal stretchers used to put a crease in blue jeans and about 4 or 5 of those were hanging on the hook, on the back of our door. We were in bed a minute or two, and this time we were really on the ends of out seats because we knew we heard something.

Suddenly, something went BOOM! . . . BOOM! . . . BOOM! and smashed the door; and these metal hangers flew off across the room!"

". . . (over the years) we've heard all kinds of noises and things that couldn't be explained as normal house creaking. My mother lives here now by herself upstairs, and we do have two apartments rented to bachelors in the back. Every once and a

Frederick Maulich (first from left), former owner and Marietta beer brewer, poses with his bartender and patrons, c. 1925. Photo courtesy of Bob Shank.

while my mother will hear a knock on her apartment door, which you have to go through two locked doors to get to. My mother refuses to open the door."

"One time my mother was lying on the sofa one night and the picture of her mom and dad hurled itself about ten feet across the room. It fell landing face up but the glass didn't break. It scared her half to death; she thought that somebody shot through the window . . . but that wasn't the case."

———————

Jack Frey, a long time friend and neighbor of the owner's father had a frightening experience involving two apparitions while he was a overnight guest in the tavern many years ago. He wrote his story down on paper and through the courtesy of Bob

Shank, Jr., who provided me with a copy, and the vivid, recorded recollections of Jack Frey, here is his account:

The following event occurred during the early morning hours of a forgotten date in the summer of 1945. I was 12 years old at the time, and the details have remained as fresh as if they transpired within the past hours.

Bob Shank (Sr.), age 24, and I had planned a fishing trip to Connowingo the following day and we decided that I would stay overnight so we could move out in the morning without any loss of time. We both turned in about 9:30 PM after getting all the necessary gear together making sure everything was in order.

It was a typical summer night, a light breeze from the west was coming through the open screened windows which I was lying next to, making it just cool enough for a light cover. The foot of the bed faced the door leading into the main hallway. To the right of Bob's side of the bed was an open door which led into another hallway going downstairs to the bar in the side room.

I recall the night being rather brilliant from the moon's radiance and consequently, the whole room was rather well lit. A person could move about without the assistance of an additional light. Something woke me up from a sound sleep. I was facing the west window, wondering what caused me to suddenly get wide awake. When all of a sudden a wave of uneasiness came over me and I distinctly remember slowly turning over to see if Bob was still asleep. He was. By positioning myself on the right side, my eyes became riveted on the door leading to the downstairs. The uneasiness prevailed, and suddenly I felt that someone was standing near that doorway.

At this time a noise reached my ears and I can only describe it as a low volume sound much like the warm evening buzzing of katydids. This sound continued unabated all throughout the event.

My heart was pounding, the sweat was pouring and my eyes locked on to that open door, knowing that something was about to happen; and happen it did!

My body was rigid with fear as the figure emerged from the doorway. I would describe what I saw generally, as a man or woman with a sheet draped over their head, totally covering their body. Now if this was the case, their body motion was not evident when walking. Here was a situation where the body motion, or the flexing of arms and legs, was absolutely not evident. Neither was the normal walking gait. The figure slowly glided or floated from that doorway into the bedroom.

My thunderous heartbeat was out of control when a second figure appeared. Keep in mind, all through this episode the subdued sound of those katydids was now becoming more intermittent. It was as if I was sensing some type of communication between those two figures.

Their forward motion was slow and I sensed that they were contemplating the room in a leisurely way. One figure was slightly taller than the other and the shroud which covered them appeared to be a dull grey color. I detected no abnormal odors at any time.

The noise continued. The figures moved or rather floated the length of the bed, one in front of the other. They were then standing at the foot of the bed looking directly at me at their closest proximity; I had turned to stone! They stood there and I couldn't detect any human form or anything that would immediately tell me that someone was playing games.

I lost all track of time as they stood there in front of me, but I was suddenly aware of an unearthly silence, the buzzing mentioned earlier had stopped. An oppressive silence of this magnitude tends to immobilize one both mentally and physically. A single thought became a trumpet in the night: "Don't do anything to alert them!".

The door at the foot of the bed slowly and silently opened. The figures hesitated and gradually exited the bedroom and just as quietly as it had opened . . . the door closed. The song of the katydids stopped.

Jack Frey
November 25, 1989

A Soldier's Cry

In April, 1917 the United States entered World War I. One young man of seventeen, who lived in rural Columbia, enlisted in the U.S. Army and was shipped overseas to fight the Germans.

It was July 1918 and the combined American and French forces started to make their first series of counter offensives attacking the Germans along a 30-mile front from Soissons to Chateau-Thierry, France. The young Columbia man was to face his first battle along that front.

That hot, July day found the young soldier's parents at home on the outskirts of Columbia; Mother was working in the kitchen and Father was seated in the outhouse probably reading a Sears catalog.

While working over the stove, his mother was surprised to hear her soldier son call her name. She quickly turned around expecting to see her boy standing behind her but found the room empty. Again, she heard him call to her, this time his voice coming from outside, through the open kitchen window.

Dropping her spoon, she rushed outside shouting to her husband, "Pop, Pop . . . did you see John, he just called to me!"

At the same time, her husband ran from the outhouse and shouted, "Mother, did you hear John call . . . he called twice!"

His mother had a foreboding feeling after that experience. She told her husband she felt something terrible had happened to their boy.

Word was received a few days later that their son was killed in action in the first few minutes of battle at Chateau-Thierry, France. His beckon from across the sea to the loved ones at home was heard at about exactly the same time that he received his wound which killed him almost instantly.

His body was not returned home; John, forever age 17, is buried in Flander's Field.[1]

The Right Name,
The Wrong Man

What's in a name? Some say the name given at birth holds powerful vibrations and in some way influences one's destiny.

Smith, Jones, Washington, each sur name is joined with one or more given names in a variety of combinations. Many parents name their sons and daughters after famous people in history. Some individuals, for business reasons, especially in the entertainment field, change their birth name to reflect a new persona, devoid of ethnic, racial or religious undertones. With millions of people in the world, it is possible that more than one individual has the same name. For instance, the most common name in the English-speaking world is Smith, with or without its variants (Smythe, Smithson, Smithfield, etc.).[1]

An Ephrata resident shared with me an unusual experience which happened to him. A very strange coincidence took place all tightly tethered to his name . . . Robert Kirkpatrick.

Mr. Kirkpatrick, age 43, works at the Aberdeen Proving Grounds in Aberdeen, Maryland. In early January of 1993, Robert Kirkpatrick had his fortune told by a physic card reader who lives about a hundred miles from the Ephrata area.

One who tells fortunes by reading cards, does just that. Each card that is "thrown" for a person merely represents events in that individual's life and it is the reader's job to accurately interpret what he sees in each card that is thrown. Just as an x-ray of an injured limb represents -in negative form- a picture of the internal bone, its usefulness to accurately pinpoint the injury is only as good as the doctor who can accurately interpret what he sees represented in the picture. If a card reader is also physic, this gives him an intuitive edge over a reader who is not. What Robert's card reader saw in his cards was frightening! In fact, according to Robert, the fortune teller said he had never seen such an unusual configuration laid before him to be interpreted.

Concerned for his safety, the reader urged him to take a leave of absence from work, for according to the cards, there would be a devastating explosion at his job which would possibly do great bodily harm to Kirkpatrick.

The Ephrata man said it would not be possible to take a leave of absence from his work but the soothsayer continued to urge him to find a way to distance himself from the job site. He suggested Kirkpatrick take a vacation, or sick leave, or even find a new job, for the cards foretold a great, imminent danger.

Kirkpatrick does general construction and maintenance work at the Proving Grounds. During the time he consulted the physic, he was involved in removing asbestos from existing structures on the site. He confessed he was growing rather weary of his work because of the huge amount of asbestos removal necessary and the long home to work commute.

Rather unnerved by the fortune tellers strong warning, he related his story to his co-workers, but felt consolation in the fact that no volatile material was in or around his job site.

On Friday, March 26, 1993, a devastating explosion rocked the New York World Trade Center in Manhattan, claiming the lives of five people. While reading newspaper accounts of the horrible explosion, Kirkpatrick was astonished to read "his own" obituary.

The New York Times, Sunday, February 28, 1993 edition identified one of the dead as: ". . . Robert Kirkpatrick, 61, a senior maintenance supervisor . . . lived in Suffern, N.Y., and had worked for the Port Authority for 12 years. He was a genial man, not one to pass up a convivial lunch with his co-workers."

Just as Ephrata's Robert Kirkpatrick had grown weary of his job, so had the deceased. The article continued: ". . . (Kirkpatrick and his co-workers) decided to have takeout food in the mechanical engineering offices. . . . When the explosion occurred, according to rescuers, the mechanical engineering offices ceased to exist. While the floor remained intact, all the walls crumbled and the ceiling collapsed. The lunchmates apparently were instantly killed by the raining concrete. . . . Though he loved his job, he had recently grown weary of his routine, his relatives said. He planned to retire in November."

Coincidence? Were the Robert Kirkpatricks, so closely linked by name and profession, more similar than anyone knows? How and why did Ephrata's Robert throw cards foretelling a complete stranger's future? Was the physic card reader more clairvoyant than even he realized using the name to bridge the gap between present and future?

What if the late Robert Kirkpatrick of Suffern, New York had had his fortune told. . .

Don't Fence Me in

Hessdale is a very small community located south of Willow Street in the southern part of Lancaster County. The population is quite small, however some inhabitants may not end up accounted for on the Federal Census. George Jones (not his real name) and his family can attest to that.

The Joneses loved their home and its peaceful surroundings, however the front door to their dwelling seemed to have a mind of its own. George Jones couldn't seem to keep their front door closed.

The door was equipped with three separate locks, but no matter how sure he was that things were bolted securely for the night, the next morning the door was open.

Of course, a whole variety of explanations ran through George's head. Thinking his six year old son might be getting up and opening the door, he asked his son to open the door. The little boy tried and tried, but the heavy door was just too much for a small child to operate.

Could it be that vandals or a vagrant were entering the house at night undetected by those sleeping upstairs? George decided to approach the problem differently. One of the locks was a tumbler type that contained a pin. George decided to close and lock the door and then break off the pin. Now it would be physically impossible to open that door even if one had a key.

The next morning, you guessed it. The door was ajar.

Mr. Jones was now totally frustrated. In desperation he decided to close the door at night but not lock it.

The next morning he arose to find the door closed. According to George: "Whoever or whatever was going through that threshold at night, did not want the door locked ... leave it unlocked and it would be closed in the morning. Lock it and it would be ajar."

That wasn't the only thing that went on in their home. Once George and his wife were sitting in the living room. The adjoining room was the dining room and this opened into the kitchen. They were startled to see movement and hear a crash as a plastic infant carrier, that had been on top of the refrigerator, flew across the kitchen and hit the floor.

No sooner than this happened, then the kitchen cabinet doors flew open. Several dishes, propelled by an unseen force, whizzed across the room and crashed against the wall.

George Jones, even after flying dishes and opened doors, still remained a skeptic, until one night when he was awakened from a sound sleep. There, in the darkness, hanging in front of him, was something he could only describe as a large piece of aluminum foil. His hair literally stood on end as he watched the vision hang suspended, rustling and sparkling as if it was reflecting some unseen light source.

George had a decided change of mind that night. He told his brother: "I have never believed in ghosts, but boy, I do now!"

The Jones family continued living in the home, taking everything in stride. Whatever or whoever it was that co-existed with them never seemed to do them any bodily harm. Mrs. Jones summed up their sentiments toward the other unseen household residents in her reply to a visiting friend. The friend, while having a cup of coffee at their dining room table asked who were the people talking in the other room. Mrs. Jones assured her guest that they were the only ones in the house.

"But I hear someone talking, I can't hear what they're saying . . . but I do hear voices," replied her friend.

"Oh, those voices . . .," smiled Mrs. Jones, ". . . well, 'those' voices are just our ghosts . . . don't pay any attention to them."

Ghostly Happenings in Southern Lancaster County

A caller from Quarryville tells of an old house she occupied for a time on Slatehill Road in East Drumore Township. She often saw shadows in spots throughout the home. On numerous occasions various objects were moved from their usual place or turned up missing only to reappear shortly later occupying the usual spot. Of course, one may say another member of the household could have moved the objects, but the woman knew for a fact no one else was in the home at the time when the objects mysteriously disappeared and then reappeared or changed location.

The same woman also told of an experience her husband had. He, at one time, lived on Kirksmill Road in Nottingham, located in the southern end of Lancaster County.

While out chopping wood in the forested area behind his house, the man was startled to hear what he thought sounded like the panting and general lip-smacking of a dog in the woods behind him. Silencing his ax he turned to see just what kind of dog was crackling the dried leaves on the forest floor and seemed, by the rustling sound, to be making a bee-line in the man's direction. To the wood-chopper's astonishment, his eyes betrayed all his other senses and beheld no dog. His ears, however, distinctly heard the snapping and cracking of brush and his eyes strained to synchronize his senses.

The invisible, noisy intruder was closing the gap between them when the woodsman beheld visual confirmation. The leaves and twigs depressed into the forest floor with every noisy foot-fall (or should I say paw-fall) of the beast. Not waiting for any more physical proof (that is fur, four paws or teeth) he ran as fast as his legs could carry him glancing back only to see the depressions made in the leaves by his noisy, panting, but invisible pursuer. Of course, the woman's husband must have set an unrecorded new world's sprinting record . . . he out ran the ghost-dog.

Double Occupancy

Esther Rumpelmyer thought the medicine her doctor pre-scribed for her was causing her to hallucinate. It started shortly after she moved into her second floor Lime Street apartment in Lancaster, Pa. in 1986.

"Everything always occurred in my bedroom," said Esther. "I usually read before I went to bed; everything was quiet, nothing unusual . . . until I turned off the light . . . then the noise started."

The noises Mrs. Rumpelmyer heard were truly a racket. Loud pounding on the doors, and walls and clanking, as if metal chains were being dragged and bounced along the floors. Imagine her surprise when lying in bed one evening, movement in her bedroom caught her attention.

She recalled: "There, standing in my room, was a woman. I would say she was in her early twenties and dressed in a skirt and blouse. Her hair was either in rollers or pin curls and tied around her head was a scarf or bandanna . . . you know, the way they used to cover their curlers . . . it was tied in the back (at the nape of the neck). She stood there for a while, just as plain as day. Then she turned and walked through the door . . . not the doorway . . . really right through the closed bedroom door. I thought I was seeing things, maybe the medicine I was taking was making me see things." Or so she thought.

Esther Rumpelmyer said unusual things went on almost every night. A man used to appear and stand at the foot of her bed and just look at her. She was never able to see this person with the detail of the woman.

"The man was usually shadowy. He was average height, and usually just stood at the foot of my bed. Then he would just disappear. . . . I only saw him about five or six times," said Esther.

Imagine how surprised she was the first night she rolled over in bed and saw the dog at her pillow. Really surprised, because Esther didn't own a dog!

"He usually slept curled up around my pillow. Sometimes he would be sitting beside the bed. He had long hair, looked a lot like a collie dog, but not a real big one . . . this went on night after night," said Esther.

Not extremely upset at the strange things she was seeing or hearing, a note from her neighbor made her re-evaluate her conclusion: "A nice young man, a college student, lived downstairs on the first floor. His bedroom was directly underneath mine. One morning I found a note in my mailbox from him. He wanted to know what in the world I was doing upstairs at one o'clock in the morning! He said it sounded like I was dragging chains around the room, or pounding nails . . . the racket was terrible. . . . I spoke to him after I got the note and told him I was in bed at one AM . . . he wanted to know how in the world I could sleep with all the noise. I told him I couldn't get to sleep . . . but I thought I was the only one hearing it. He assured me he heard it too."

That conversation with her neighbor changed the way Mrs. Rumpelmyer viewed life in her apartment as she knew it. Obviously, if both heard the same thing, Mrs. Rumpelmyer wasn't hallucinating.

Now she was a bit frightened. Her son even suggested that a priest be called in to bless the place. Esther, however, objected. She had also talked to her daughter about the situation and tended to agree with her. She and her daughter had reasoned: in all this time, the people and animal in her room never harmed her. Why should she only be frightened now?

Esther had other experiences in her apartment. Sometimes the light on her night stand would turn on. She would turn it off; it would go back on. She'd turn it off, back on it would go. The same thing would happen with her radio and her clock alarm.

"Finally I gave up and just pulled out the plug(s) (of the various appliances)," said Esther.

Also unnerving were the voices. On several occasion she'd hear a woman's voice cry: "Rose, no . . . no don't . . . Rose. . . ."

A co-worker who Mrs. Rumpelmyer confided in said that there might be an explanation for the haunting. According to her friend there had been a fire there and a woman died in the fire. Was this the spirit of the young woman whose life ended so tragically?

Closer examination of her room revealed the top panes of her bedroom window were blackened or scorched. The discoloration was permanent and could not be removed by cleaning. Esther does not know what year the fire might have occurred.

I, as a writer and researcher, decided to do some checking. According to the Lancaster Fire Bureau's records (covering the years 1880-mid 1956) found at the Lancaster County Historical Society, the Lancaster Fire Department answered six separate fire calls to that address between the years 1928 and 1956. Apparently these fires were of no consequence because no reference to them is made in the local newspapers around the time frame of the dates in question. The next 26 years are a matter for speculation, as record keeping stopped mid 1956 and only resumed about 1982. Unable to sort through approximately 9,500 newspaper editions between that time gap . . . verification of a fire is still pending.

The fact remains that Mrs. Rumpelmyer knows what strange things went on in her Lime Street apartment, as does her former neighbor.

From the very day in 1992 when Esther Rumpelmyer moved out of her apartment, she has never seen or heard anything unusual in her daily life even though she still takes the same prescribed medication.

As for the second floor apartment on Lime Street . . . it's still there and presently occupied with new tenants . . . and maybe a few old ones too.

---

*Editor's Note: The source for this story (Double Occupancy) wishes to keep the exact location of the apartment and her identity anonymous. Therefore, Esther Rumpelmyer is a fictitious name. All other facts and dates surrounding this story are true.

A Woman of Her Word

"L'il Nanny" was a tiny lady with a heart as big as all outdoors. Her sweet face was softly framed in a halo of wispy, white hair which gave her an almost ethereal appearance. Loved and respected by all her family, she in her 93 years, had cuddled and loved each new addition to the clan as if they were her own.

Mary Catherine Henry and Joanne M. Kraybill, two of her great grandchildren, spent several hours one afternoon telling me about their grandmother and some very strange occurrences.

According to Mary and Joanne, L'il Granny spoke with a thick Italian accent. Mary, like most children, could be rather contrary at times. L'il Nanny in disapproval, would often shake her finger at Mary and good naturedly scold her saying: "MAR EE AH, I'MA GONNA CUMA BACK AFFA I'MA DEAD TO SEEYA YOU!" Little did Mary realize then, how prophetic L'il Nanny's words were.

L'il Nanny passed away in December of 1972. The night of the funeral the family members gathered at Joanne's home, an old log cabin (now modernized) located along the Fruitville Pike in Lancaster. Finding solace in companionship, Joanne and Mary and several others bedded down for the night, all occupying one large room.

Joanne recounted what happened next: "I thought everybody was sleeping ... my cousin Marion was sleeping. My other cousins were sleeping; nobody was making a noise. I thought, 'Well, I'll go to sleep (too).' So I laid on my side, and then I turned (to the left). And then I saw it! I saw this black little figure at the door. (Then) my heart went THUMPTY THUMP and I laid on my back and thought 'Oh My!' As I rolled over to my right side I had the covers up to my neck, just about over my head . . . I was SO SCARED! I heard the floor boards creak . . . and then it (the creaking) stopped. So then I got brave and looked over to my left and saw the little figure go over to the bed where Mary's two sisters were sleeping. The figure leaned over at my cousin's bed. The little lady was all in black, like a veil, completely covered. I knew it was her (L'il Nanny), I knew it because whenever anyone stayed over night L'il Nanny would go over to you at night and say "BELLA, BELLA" or beautiful baby (in Italian)."

Terrified, Joanne rolled back to her right side clutching her blankets as she heard the creaking coming over to her side of the room. She felt a tremendous pressure on the top of her head, and thought she was up against the headboard . . . but she wasn't as she finally peeked after a considerable amount of time passed.

Joanne thought she was the only witness to the event, although she had tried desperately to wake her bed partner by pulling her hair, pinching and scratching her.

The next morning she asked her wounded and bruised comrad why she didn't wake up and displayed a hank of hair she had snatched from the head of the sound sleeper.

In surprise, her cousin Mary Henry, who had occupied the bed on the first stop of Nanny's child checking round said that she was awakened by a very heavy pressure on her leg. This was a familiar sensation . . . since Nanny would often grab her leg in the same way when she was alive and on her rounds at night. She assured Joanne she had seen the same black figure, saw the figure go to Joanne's bed, but thought everyone else was sleeping. She too thought it was Nanny . . . coming back, just like she always said she would.

Two months after Nanny's death she appeared to another member of the family. Mary Henry's mother usually came home during her lunch hour to eat. While preparing a sandwich, she heard the familiar Italian phrase, Nanny always called her with for lunch, 'Marion, mange.' As she watched in sheer amazement, a small, white figure turned and floated to the end of the kitchen. She (Nanny) then proceeded down the stairs into the dining room and over to the chair which had been her favorite in life. Then she disappeared.

Could it be that L'il Nanny who so loved her family in life transcended the veil of death to be with them again? Not only was she a loving Mother . . . she was also a woman of her word.

Walking Around Money

Harvey Hickson and his wife moved into their home located along Third Street in Columbia in May of 1990. It stands in stately elegance, snuggled against several other houses similar in appearance.

Almost a year had passed when something odd happened to Mr. Hickson. He explained it was the summer of 1991 when he went to the local MAC machine to withdraw $60.00 in cash. He then stopped to buy gas, putting the change back into his wallet. Arriving home, he followed his usual routine, at night placing his wallet on the bedroom dresser.

A new day dawned. Dressing, he of course picked up his wallet, and through habit checked to see it contained the amount he knew should be there. Much to his surprise, $20.00 was missing.

Harvey Hickson said, "I knew exactly how much money was in my wallet. I knew the amount I started with, I knew exactly how much I spent, and I knew how much I had returned to my wallet. Twenty dollars was gone."

Thinking his wife might have needed the money, he asked her. No, she hadn't taken it.

Still puzzled, he dismissed the episode. Until the same thing happened again. He recalled: ". . . I thought I was going nuts. I couldn't even take care of my own money anymore."

Not long after the second episode, his wife's friend stopped to visit. The friend had grown up in the house, in fact the Hicksons had purchased the property from her parents. He told her about the money disappearing from his wallet, could there be a way a thief might get in that he didn't know about?

The friend listened quietly and said her mother had had a

similar problem. According to her, back in the 70's, her mother called the children together to find out who had taken money from her "stash". Like a lot of people, the Mother would occasionally hide a little "mad money" under a plate in the top cupboard shelf. The payroll turned up short! Who took it? Every one in the house said they never touched it. The now grown daughter still avows today that this is the truth.

The friend also told of a hair raising experience that happened to her brother in his bedroom located in the converted attic. He was laying on his bed one night when he heard what sounded like his keys jingling. The key ring was placed on his dresser across the room. Breathless, he listened as the sound of slow scraping came from the direction of the dresser. Then, CRASH!, his keys landed on the floor.

Startled, he examined his dresser and the fallen keys. Oddly enough, a trail in the dust stretched the length of the dresser top indicating the route the keys traveled.

The Hicksons found the tales interesting, especially the one about the missing money. Harvey felt reassured he may not be losing his mind after all.

Some time had passed since the money disappeared. Harvey said his wife was taking a college course. She was at class and Harvey was sitting in the living room, his only company being the family dog, a beagle.

Quite suddenly, the dog jumped to his feet and started barking. Harvey thought there might be someone at the door, for the beagle was carrying on wildly.

Harvey explained what happened next: "I got up to answer the door and as I took one step away from my chair, I went through a funnel of HOT air, face first . . . just like wind out of a hot furnace. It was almost like a static field and HOT! It was gone as quickly as I went through it. I stood for a minute trying to figure out what happened. Then I took a step back, a step to center, then sideways, then back . . . all around, trying to locate it again. All the time our beagle was barking wildly."

Mr. Hickson then opened the front door looking for, well, anyone. He even walked around the house but there was no one outside.

Shortly after this happened, he returned home to find the

iron was on, and hot, and no one was home. When his wife arrived he scolded her, but much to his chagrin, she hadn't used the iron nor had she even been near it.

Harvey Hickson had a hunch. He had a feeling some one died in the home. But it was just a hunch. Between the time he decided to do some background research on their home, and the time he actually checked the old records, they had a new addition to the family, a lovely little Border Collie. The little female bundle of fur needed a name and after several days of contemplation, the Hicksons decided on the name "Emma" - perfect.

Following up on his hunch, he first consulted Mrs. Edna Clark, local historian, who provided him with nineteenth century background information, even the name of the architect. Then at Lancaster County Courthouse Archives he turned up some very interesting facts.

The house dated back to 1899. In 1920 Mr. and Mrs. Paul Sills bought the property. In 1945 the property was sold by the Sills to the family from whom the Hicksons bought it.

Checking old newspaper obituaries, Harvey Hickson found some proof his hunch may have been correct. According to the newspaper archives, Mrs. Sills died. Whether or not she expired in the home is a matter for speculation. Husband Paul Sills became ill. He was then admitted to a veteran's hospital where he later died.

Were the strange occurrences caused by the spirit of a former owner, trapped in time and space? Harvey Hickson says his wife was and is afraid of the strange things that happen. Harvey, however, is not.

If the house *is* haunted by the spirit of the deceased former owner, the Hicksons just may be communicating on a daily basis with her. For every time they call their little Border Collie, they call their ghost. You see, the late Mrs. Sills' name was . . . EMMA.

Acknowledgments

My heartfelt thanks goes to Bob and Florence Miller. Bob, a fine journalist and photographer, dug through his personal files to provide me with information and photographs I might otherwise never obtained. His news articles about my planned book were invaluable. Thank you very much.

Florence, his wife, and acting President of the Columbia Historic Preservation Society, gave her time and energy in opening up the society's *Columbia News* microfilm for my research. She also provided story leads and continuing encouragement. Thank you Florence.

Thanks also to John Crawford, who's interest and story leads were greatly appreciated.

A special thanks to Mrs. Edna Clark. A lovely lady and a brilliant historian. Thank you for letting me glimpse into your knowledge of the past and your ghostly experiences.

I would also like to thank Gregory A. Coco, who graciously permitted me to use his story, "A Mysterious Visitor" as it appeared in his very enjoyable book, *On The Bloodstained Field II, 132 More Human Interest Stories Of The Campaign and Battle Of Gettysburg,* Thomas Publications, Gettysburg, Pa. 1989. Thank you very much.

To all the people who called me, wrote to me, visited or permitted me to come into their homes, I thank you. This book was only possible because of you.

My sister, Bette Jean Crouse, will never know how much she encourages me in every thing I do. She's always the first to nudge me with her elbow and get me going. Thanks Bette.

And thank you to my wonderful husband Sam, he is truly . . . the wind beneath my wings.

FOOTNOTES

To My Mother

1. Peale, Norman Vincent. *Not Death At All*. Prentice-Hall, Inc., 70 Fifth Avenue, New York, New York. 1948, 1949. p. 22.

Introduction

1. Jones, Louis C.. *Things That Go Bump In The Night*. Syracuse University Press., 1983.
2. Nesbitt, Mark. *Ghosts of Gettysburg. Spirits, Apparitions and Haunted Places of The Battlefield*. Thomas Publications. Gettysburg, Pa. 1991. p.11.
3. Aurand, A. Monroe, Jr. *The "Pow-Wow" Book*. The Aurand Press. Harrisburg, Pa. 1929. p. 79.
4. Adams, George Worthington. *Doctors In Blue. The Medical History Of The Union Army In The Civil War*. Morningside Press., Dayton, Ohio. 1985. p. 127.
5. Ibid., 50.

A Few Words About Ghosts and Haunted Houses

1. Crisp, Marty. "Houses With 'Haunted' Past Difficult To Sell?", *Sunday News, Lancaster, Pa*. 25 October 1992.
2. Ibid.
3. Ibid.
4. Brodeur, Nicole. "For Ghost Hunter Spirits Are Real", *The Express Line - West - Lancaster, Pa*. 18 November 1992.
5. Ibid.
6. Ibid.
7. Crisp, Marty. "Houses With 'Haunted' Past Difficult to Sell?", *Sunday News, Lancaster, Pa*. 25 October 1992.
8. Smith, Susy. *Prominent American Ghosts*. The World Publishing Co., Cleveland, Ohio, 1967. p. 75.
9. Ibid., 80.
10. Ibid., 80.

Albert Einstein on the Mysterious

1. Van Over, Raymond. *Unfinished Man*. The World Publishing Company. New York, 1972. p. 61.

Man's Best Friend

Personal interview with eye witness by author, 1976.

Miss Mary Mifflin of Norwood

1. Sneath, E. Hershey. *America's Greatest Sonneteer*. Clover Press. Columbia, Pa. 1925.

Personal interview with eye witness by author, 1975.

Columbia's Haunted Museum

Personal interview with eye witnesses, 1993.

The Visitor

Appears in its entirety by written permission of author Gregory A. Coco from his book, *On The Bloodstained Field II, 132 More Human Interest Stories Of The Campaign and Battle Of Gettysburg,* Thomas Publications, Gettysburg, Pa. 1989.

The Ironville Airship

Anonymous contributor. Telephone interview by author, 26 January 1993.

The Legend of the Headless Horseman

Local Legend

Mystery Blast and Falling Ice

1. *The Columbia, Pa., News.* Wed., 31 July 1957.
2. *The Columbia, Pa., News.* Tues., 6 August 1957.
3. *The Columbia, Pa., News.* Wed., 31 July 1957.
4. Ibid.
5. Ibid.
6. Vara, John. "Taking Your Chances An Examination Of Risk Assessment And The Psychology Of Worry", *The Old Farmer's Almanac 1994.* Yankee Publishing Incorporated. 1993. p. 220.
7. Ibid.
8. *The Lancaster New Era.* "Space Junk: Hubble's Solar Panel Dumped In Earth Orbit". Lancaster, Pa., 7 December 1993. p.1.
9. Ibid., p. A-5.

An Eerie Old House in New Texas

1. Bette Atkinson. Telephone interview by author, 19 February 1993. Transcript in hand of Bette Atkinson to author 20 February 1993.

Witch Trial in Pennsylvania

1. *Authentic history of Lancaster County, In The State Of Pennsylvania.* J.I. Mombert, D.D., J.E. Barr & Co., 1869, Reprinted Southwest Pennsylvania Genealogical Services, Laughlintown, Pennsylvania, 1988. p. 59.
2. Aurand, A. Monroe. *The Realness of Witchcraft In America.* The Aurand Press, Harrisburg, Penna. 1942. p. 17.
3. Ibid.
4. Ibid.

The Goat

Anonymous Contributor. Taped personal interview by author, 20 January 1993.

The Haunted Mill House

Karen D., Transcript (typed) in hand of Karen D. to author 24 June 1993.

The Girls of Kinderhook

1. Ellis, Franklin & Steven, Samuel. *History Of Lancaster County Pennsylvania.* Everts and Peck, Philadelphia. 1883. p. 882.
2. Ibid.
3. Ibid.
Personal recollection and files of author.

Chicques Hill Haunting

1. Swiger, Anna M., Chairman, Historic Research Committee. *Columbia, Pennsylvania. Its People-Culture, Religions, Customs, Education, Vocations, Industry. From Shawanah Indian Town, 1726 To Columbia, 1976.* 1977. p. 3.
2. John C. Musser. "Despite A Full Moon, Ghost Shuns Chickies Last Night". *The Columbia, Pa. News.* 28 August 1969.
3. John C. Musser. "Penitent Youths Confess To Hoax". *The Columbia, Pa. News.* 29 August 1969.
4. *The Columbia, Pa. News.* 28 August 1969.
5. Ibid.
6. Ibid.
7. Ibid.

Shanks Tavern in Marietta

Bob Shank. Taped interview by author 30 March 1993.

A Soldier's Cry

Author's personal files.

The Right Name, The Wrong Man

1. Lambert, Eloise and Pei, Mario. *Where They Came From And What They Mean.* Lotahropo, Lee & Shepard Co., Inc., New York. 1960. p. 98.

Robert Kirkpatrick. Telephone interview by author Spring 1993.

Don't Fence Me in

Anonymous contributor. Telephone interview by author November 1993.

Ghostly Happenings in Southern Lancaster County

Anonymous contributor. Telephone interview by author Spring 1993.

Double Occupancy

Esther Rumpelmyer (pseud.), telephone interview by author, December, 1993.

A Woman of Her Word

Mrs. Joanne Caterbone, Joanne Kraybill, Mary Catherine Henry, taped interview by author, 11 December 1993, Lancaster, Pa.

Walking Around Money

Harvey Hickson (pseud.) telephone interview by author December 1993.

About the Author

Dorothy Burtz Fiedel was born in Columbia, Pennsylvania. She graduated cum laude from Millersville University, Millersville, Pa. with a bachelor of science degree.

She is married and the mother of two sons, and is currently working on a second collection of haunted places in Lancaster County, Pennsylvania.